SONGS OF MIST AND RAIN

A collection of poems

POETRY FROM NORTH BENGAL

JOITA GANGULY

ink Scribe

ink

Songs of Mist And Rain

Publisher: Inkscribe Publishing Pvt. Ltd.

ISBN Number: 978-1-969259-11-1

Dedication

I dedicate this book to my beloved parents, Lt. Arun Kumar Ganguly and Lt. Meera Ganguly, whose unwavering inspiration has been the driving force behind my writing since childhood.

I'm also deeply grateful to the breathtaking landscapes of North Bengal, particularly the Darjeeling mountains and Dooars, where I spent my formative years surrounded by the serene beauty of tea gardens. The nostalgia of those days resonates deeply in many of my poems.

Special thanks to Abhi for your constant inspiration, which has been a guiding force in my creative journey.

And to Mrinal, my heartfelt gratitude for your patience and understanding, for indulging my quirks and letting me have my way – with love.

Forward

For Joita Ganguly's **SONGS OF MIST AND RAIN**

It's rare to find a voice that can whisper and still carry thunder. Joita Ganguly's poems do just that. They speak softly—often with the clarity of a single image, the hush of a fog-covered hillside, the scent of tea leaves crushed between fingers— and yet they resound with history, fracture, and quiet defiance.

Reading this collection is like walking through a forest of echoes: women's footsteps, forgotten gods, rivers that remember, stones that resist. Joita does not impose her voice upon the page—she listens to it. Her lines are pared down, but never hollow. They carry the weight of unspoken things. And when she speaks of grief, of protest, of love or myth, she does so not from abstraction but from the ground up. These are poems rooted in the soil—Darjeeling mist, Dooars shadows, postcolonial tremors, a mother's kitchen, a burnt page, a mountain that refuses translation.

What moves me most is how her poetry turns away from spectacle. There is no performance of pain here. No indulgence in despair. Instead, we find precision, patience, and presence. Even in her most political lines, Joita leans into lyric, not slogan. Her resistance is textured, often intimate— a woman standing still in the middle of a storm, a child eavesdropping on the silence between two generations, a poem scratched onto stone where paper has failed.

In an age of noise, these poems ask us to listen.

And listening, here, is not passive—it's a form of survival. The serene music that her poems bear is something to be felt from within.

It is a privilege to walk beside this collection, to witness what Joita holds, and what she releases.

— Kajari Ghosh
1ST. July 2025
Siliguri, Darjeeling

Preface

To Stand Where the River Turns

This collection began not as a book, but as a slow gathering—of silences, questions, inheritances, and echoes. Some poems arrived like mist, others like verdicts. Many came from walking—through tea gardens in the hills, through city streets slick with slogans, through the half-lit corridors of personal and collective memory.

Here, language carries its bruises. It listens to stone, to streams, to women's footsteps on forgotten paths. Sometimes it murmurs in myth; sometimes it protests. These poems do not shout, but they remember. They are steeped in landscapes both inner and outer—rivers that shift their names, mountains that keep ancestral grief, hands that etch meaning where it is not meant to stay.

There is no single narrative here, only a pulse: of migration and return, of fracture and faith. These are poems for those who carry history in their breath and still dare to name tenderness political.

If you find a fragment of your own reflection here—in the still water, in the chipped wall, in a word half-swallowed—let it be a conversation. I believe poetry is not an answer. It is a gesture toward listening.

— Joita Ganguly

About The Author

Joita Ganguly was born in early sixties in North Bengal. Being the daughter of a renowned tea planter Arun Kumar Ganguly, she spent her formative years in the tea gardens of Darjeeling and Dooars. After her post graduation in English literature from the University of North Bengal, she took up the job of a teacher of English in a Dooars girls' school where he spent thirty-two years of her working life moulding the tea garden girls into formidable toiling women, conscious of their self-respect. The struggle of the subalterns, tea garden workers especially the women folk sculpted the author into a voice of the deprived and the humiliated. This book bears the strokes of some of her inner self.

— Shirsha Chakraborty

Contents

Midnight Bell

The bell tolls in the dead of night
At the boys' hostel door.
The owl's hoot thickens the dark,
While something stirs—a subtle trace
Drawn in the blackened grass.
A rat.

The half-moon hangs, caught like a hook
In the tall Dalbergia's limbs.
Crickets sustain a tremulous tune
For Nature's ear.
And the wind—
It whispers of tomorrow's food chain.

Paralysis

Her eyes shone like lanterns in the night,

The Bastard Teak Forest bloomed with hairy petals bright,

Each touch a whisper of insidious intent,

A seduction that her lips seemed to invent.

Locks framed her face, a mosaic of light and shade,

Dancing on her eyelids, a gentle parade,

Her slender neck descended, a path untold,

Into the cleavage where ancient secrets unfold.

The journey of passion moved with stealthy pace,

But her paralyzed spine remained a frozen space,

Unable to respond, a body locked in time,

A heart that yearned, yet limbs that couldn't align.

Yearning

Come, sweetheart, as twilight deepens slow,

One by one, the lights begin their gentle glow,

Like distant stars, they weave a tender spell,

Crafting the garment of my love that'll wrap you well,

Warming the haven of my humble home, where love will dwell.

My gaze spreads like a carpet on your path, a warm invite,

My ears, attuned to every sound, await your gentle stride,

The rhythm of your anklets, a melody so sweet,

With arms outstretched, yearning, my heart skips a beat.

The cherry blooms in the gentle breeze of your breath,

Fragrance wafts, touching the restless sea to calmness and depth,

Above, the constellations burst into a wild, cosmic dance,

As you draw near, my love, and my heart finds its trance.

Night Feels the Pull of Darkness

The darkness can decrypt the mystery of the rib-caged night.

The stars know this secret.

Thus, the verdant darkness remains silent.

Water makes its home within water, and silently slips away

The young dragonfly, with the habit

of three hundred million years

Of traversing the earth, pushes water with its breath.

Life's journey unfolds in wild arum and reeds.

On the branch of a Dalbergia,

That has shed its leaves, hangs

a moon smeared with mist.

An owl flies and perches nearby.

In the grassy woods, a young mouse hides.

O Ophelia!

You don't know, Ophelia—

Every door in this palace whispers,

If I close one, who will die,

And who will smile, holding a death warrant.

That day, when rain fell in your hair,

I thought—God still paints.

Your voice was like a gentle dusk,

A place where sin dared not enter.

But why did you choose them?

Were you truly afraid of me?

Or did their shadows smother the light in your love?

Did I ask too much?

I only longed for you to say:

"Not everything is a lie, Hamlet—

I'm here."

I sought refuge in you.

I thought your smile

Would banish every shadow.

But you were silent.

You never asked, Ophelia—

How I learned to lie while staring into eyes.

You never stopped me to say,

"Where are you heading to, Hamlet,

With all this fire in your chest?"

In the palace corridors, deception hides,

Wearing masks of loyalty.

Those who love are the easiest prey.

You, Ophelia, were that simple poem.

I thought you'd save me.

And you?

You sent spies to find conspiracy in my words.

Even in your love, there was fear,

A duty to your father—

And I too carried the same burden.

So I stood, torn between staying and leaving.

That's when you turned everything back,

Returned my faith in the constant star,

The love comparable to the sun's fiery truth,

Which was more than the love of forty thousand brothers.

But you never understood my love.

You trusted their voices over mine—

They who never saw the tears behind my rage,

Only saw an unfinished revenge of a prince

Why didn't you see,

How I wake up at night, my father's shadow beside me?

Exhausted, I say, "I can't, Ophelia."

Why didn't you reach out then?

I didn't write sonnets for you,

I carved open my chest.

Wrote you in blood—

"You're the only one who knows who I am beneath this crown."

But you listened to them.

One by one,

they cut away every hand I could hold.

They want me mad,

They want me loveless.

Yes, I said— "Get thee to a nunnery",

Because I was more afraid of my own love than of you.

How can someone who sleeps with doubt every night, love?

So I'm alone, devastated, speechless.

And so I stood, watching,

As a love slowly entered its grave.

When you went into the water,

Did your bird-like hands tremble?

Did you whisper my name?

Or was that name like a promise lost in the air,

Just a promise

That never made it past your lips?

Your silence can bring down a kingdom.

You left, floating on the water—

I don't know if my name was still on your lips.

I don't know if you looked up at the sky for the last time,

Searching for me.

Today I know—

love is more than two people.

It needs time, courage,

Sometimes rebellion.

But you didn't rebel, Ophelia.

You chose silence.

And now—

The world is at peace,

But there's a war inside me.

I don't want a crown, Ophelia,

I just want to know—

Was love that fragile?

Or did we both lose to time?

Today I'm not a king, nor a lover—

I'm just a question living inside a dead heart—

If you were here, could I have been human?

Awaiting

A serene face,

bathed in the soft light

of sacred chants and ancient hymns.

But behind the veil, a demonic frenzy churns.

Since then, I've feared hymns and prayers,

For goodness now stands uncertain,

Silent and still, with a worried soul.

Seven sleeping men lie within a cave;

A dog keeps silent vigil at the entrance.

On the ridges of distant hills,

humans still work the land—

worn hands growing weaker,

Bent backs bending further,

In a striving

To make all clear eyes disappear.

So that no pure eyes can see.

Even clarity now feels dangerous—

for too often,

the pure become the storm.

And so,

Life—alongside seven companions—

Waits

For the exploitation of faith

To end.

Association

When I see the sky turn blue,

It is Autumn that I am reminded of.

The bushy Kans grass blooming along the river bank,

The faint scent of the twilight blossom Parijat,

Resplendent with land lotus, the aura of the earth

Speaks of festivals. The scent of new clothes

Drifts to my nose

And the rumbling of drums reaches my ears.

Well-dressed couples walk past,

Spreading fragrance as they go.

Seeing their hands intertwined,

The universe rejoices in eternal delight.

Then as if the tuberose scented,

Then as if the sound of shehnai plays,

Then hope, faith, and

The song of life spread throughout the world.

How strange these connections are.

The poet calls it golden shower tree,

Some says it is blooming cassia,

But whenever I see yellow flowers,

Oh girl, I am reminded only of you.

(For You, Abhaya)

Endless

Touching the wall of silence,

Graffiti of words.

Above the ruins, the sky — indifferent and blue,

It knows that destruction speaks only of prosperity.

Absence conveys

The truth of presence.

Do the unblinking eyes of time

Ever veiled?

In the face of countless galaxies

Where do I stand?

In this world resonating with eternal abundance

Existence is perpetual.

(Courtesy: Octavio Paz)

In the Forest

Upon the breast of Murti's quiet stream
There lies a veil of soft and tender light,
As dew of winter settles on the field,
Along its edge, in language earth has known—
Unlettered, yet as eloquent as song.

The sky above, so full of speechless thought,
Looks down with eyes that touch the river's soul
And breathes upon its waves a golden warmth.
The breath, like sunlight wrapped in woven mist,
Now brushes close against the waiting heart.

The hidden truths that dwell behind sylvan walls
Have made their home beside the flowing grace.
And from the deep green hush the forest calls,

Its shadowed arms stretched out in silent signs,

To draw the spirit nearer to the dark

Where meaning stirs beneath the moss and bark.

The soil, aware, begins to fill the mind—

With musings deep, like roots that drink from stars,

And in that breath — so slow, so vast, so still —

The thought becomes a forest of its own.

My Happiness

Where can be my little dog?
Where must my little dog be?
I searched for him inside the house
I searched for him impatiently.

I didn't see him on the couches,
A place on which he often lies.
Not the place he often slouches
For the sparrow who pecks and flies.

Where can be my sweet li'l Pook?
I couldn't guess where he could jouk,
He's the single star in my sky,
But I can't find him and I cry.

My heart aches as I want to hold
Him tightly on my pining chest.
All my feelings now go so cold
As I begin to sink in angst.

Then I chanced to see a wheatish stir
In lazy stretch b'neath the cushions,
My boy is sleeping with the pillows
With the linen in gold fusion

He didn't listen to my calls, his
Mischiefs he is so famous for.
He licked my nose so lovingly
None can be angry any more.

All our happ'ness is strewn around us.
Just go out once and find them thus.

Waiting....

" Wait", he had said

Beyond the telephone.... black?

May be.

May be not.

But she did.

Waited.

Under the branches that

Simpered

Under their leafy banner.

Cloud rose from the valley

To caress the mighty rock

With moistening embrace

And took the wet from her eyelids

To meld it in the fog.

Waited...

And she ....

The autumnal breeze

Glided the leaves

Down to her feet

The maple reddened....

Blue pine cushioned her feet

As she ....

Waited.

The telephone.... black

May be.

May be not.

Didn't ring

Barks advanced.

Her own true family

Fusing into ....

"Ted Hughes", she thought.

The telephone

Black....

It had rung only once.

The Scar

In hushed blue lotus-bind

Cavernous silence...

Consciousness dissolving, head submerged.

Nocturnal substrate of futile desire

Cuts sharp as razor-trace.

Piercing with keen talons

Retreating memory's ghost.

Pressed against breast with profound tenderness

A bloodied needle.

Seeping crimson

Fragments of reality's raw self

Overwhelms all sensation.

Yet—

The darkest wing of night
Ensures obsidian passage in
the night bird's churning dark
That ensures the coming of dawn,
in eternal desire.

Festival

There'll be festivals doubled, tripled —

drums pounding in neon, speakers vomiting joy —

protests drowned in foam, demands dissolving in synthetic colours —

Why burn the truth when illusion blazes better?

We'll scrub every shame with champagne laughter,

we'll baptize blame in beer, rinse guilt with rum.

Life will float — plastic on the pleasure tide —

anger evaporating in vodka shots —

fashion parades down the capitalist runway,

mascara'd grief on discount display —

take the trip, take the selfie, take whatever the hell you want!

Raise hell, all night, all day —

find your peace in pre-rolled desire,

we'll inject you with endless highs,

forget the bite of the conscience-rat in your chest —

don't think, don't stop, don't ache —

just drink, just dance, just vanish in light.

(For you, Abhaya)

Howl for a Dying Man

The man was dying—

dying like rust in a gutter, like smoke curling from a cigarette stub in the ashtray of God,

he had sent his daughter to school, yes, to school! to learn letters and numbers and dreams—

but she came back riding a broken bicycle and clutching a thousand rupees like dead flowers,

the school disappeared—evaporated—

no teachers, no students, no chalk dust, no flags fluttering in morning assemblies—

the last bell never rang.

She never took her exam, never saw a hall ticket,

was told to go to another school, but it was too far

and the bicycle wheezed like a dying cow, and money was a myth

so the wheels never turned again.

The man had a son too—

same dream, same hope flickering like neon in a blackout,

he went to school, came back with six hundred rupees and a look of confusion.

No English, no science, no math,

just empty periods echoing through cement halls.

So he vanished—Kerala!

followed two elder boys into the belly of another state—

sent cash like lifeblood wrapped in envelopes,

that cash bought the man medicine from the steel drawers of a government hospital—

but the pills were laced with something vile,

the man's breath stopped mid-word, mid-prayer, mid-regret.

The wife—the woman of cracked feet and calloused palms—

carried bricks on her spine, stirred cement with other forgotten wives,

until the canal behind the neighbourhood bloomed red

and the daughter was found like a discarded doll in the thicket,

blood flowering from between her legs, skull split open like an unripe coconut.

No one heard the scream.

The wife went mad.

Eyes rolled in directions language could not follow.

She laughed at birds, cursed the wind, wept into iron plates.

But the boy returned—O survivor of borrowed states!

Wearing grease and silence,

found a job in a garage, fingers slick with the underbelly of machines.

He cares for his mother now—feeds her rice, wraps her in blankets of memory,

and at night—

he walks out into the smoke-hissed city

with a spanner in his hand,

and his eyes—they say—

his eyes burn like tigers who remember everything.

Why

It's your fault, Vidyasagar—

Why did you show me letters,

Open my eyes to script and sky,

Turn my face toward the light—

Only to leave me staring into shadow?

You said: "Because you are human,

You too shall have a name."

Not— "You are woman, he is man,"

Not that tired frame.

And I believed you.

I made a vow to rise,

Crossed oceans, touched the stars,

Flew beyond the narrowing skies.

I've borne the wounded from the field,
Wielded strength with trembling grace.
I drive the plane, the train,
The cab, the bus—I take my place.

Everywhere, I walk beside him,
Step for step, breath for breath—
Shoulder to shoulder,
Equal in life, and even in death.

Then tell me—
Why must I stay behind
When the shift turns to night?
Is your courage afraid of the dark—
Or only of my light?

(After Abhaya)

Clamour in the Humid Silence

Rain fell this afternoon—

not renewal,

but a gesture of forgetting.

A benediction for the broken spine

of the violated woman,

whose body lies like a question unanswered—

death, a drizzle upon her scalded flesh.

The vapour hangs—

sweat of the crushed season,

not unlike the stench of conquest,

the heat of a body without conscience,

pressing its weight

on the backs of all breathing things.

This, not a storm,
but an argument with silence.
The rain arrives like a sentence
without subject or grammar,
cool, indifferent,
like the final frost
that closes the wound without healing.

And I—
threadbare thinker in this fetid dusk—
consider the paradox of endings.
Life is not chill,

not a twilight retreat into cottony ash.
Life begins in the wound of light,
in the unbearable glare of morning.

So why this pilgrimage toward frost?
What longing moves us
toward the blank spaces
where nothing bleeds,

nothing breathes?

The soul—unsheltered—sobs beneath its breath.
No anthem can soothe this fever.
No doctrine can carry
the weight of that gaze—
those eyes that have begun
to weep blood
instead of tears.

(For you, Abhaya)

Trees by the Water

The Hijol tree stands alone by the water.
Nothing dramatic. Just there.
Behind it, evening falls—
not like a curtain,
but like fatigue on the back of a man
who's been digging a ditch too long.

Mist rises without apology.
The sky scratches its blue skin.
And the bamboo—somewhere behind—
makes a sound.
Not singing. Not speaking.
Something between pressure and surrender.

A bird without a name

sits in the korch tree—

its wings smell faintly of algae and wet stone.

The duckweed floats like thin excuses.

On it, something old rests—

a prayer maybe,

but crusted over in mud

like everything else.

People say trees are silent.

They are wrong.

Trees wait.

For rain. For wind. For the moment

when they will fly.

Yes, fly—why not?

A drooping branch knows

what it cost the root to hold still.

Water doesn't reflect,

it dissects.

Cuts the world into moving shapes—

broken, and too honest.

Leaves fly off like insects.
Water breaks like glass—
quiet, and total.

The trees see peace.
They do not enter it.
Korch petals fall
and cling to the wild rice,
as if they want to be eaten.

And the hijol tree laughs—
sharp, like a snapped twig—
"Go on, fool.

Go far.
No one waits in this water.
No one stays."

Call

I once had a field.

Now, I no longer see it.

The shiuli tree that scattered white stars

across my courtyard—

vanished, along with the courtyard itself.

And that tree?

It knew when winter came,

Shedding its leaves like memory.

By Dol, it dressed in tender green,

like hope returned too late.

I wonder—

does it remember me?

The Teak blossoms
hid their faces in my hair

At the slightest breeze.
Now, my hair holds only
the stillness of afternoons.

Windows are latched.
Doors sealed.
Lest the sky comes looking.

Where has the blood-orange sunset fled?
Into what exile
have all the edges and gaps disappeared?

Behind every crevice,
a mechanical chill hums.
I fill my lungs
with borrowed air—
sterile, indifferent.
Somewhere between silence and static,

I've forgotten

how to answer

the call

of the living earth.

Thirst

I lift cupped hands to lips,
and offer libation
With the blood of my heart.

At noon, lost on a road that melts into pitch,
I cross barefoot,
each step searing.

Mistaking heat for water,
I chase the shadowed mirage—
again, again.

Longing haunts me,

lurking in every narrow lane,
wherever I try to hide.

A silent consciousness
whistles from some far shore,
calling me
to respond
to the summons of bottomless waters—
and yet I search
for a crack
in the hard prison of safety.

I bury the storm's wail
in the deep embrace
of feigned slumber.

And still—
I watch the ants,
marching in line,
in search of sweetness.

To You, Girl — A Whisper to the Wind

Where do you wander, girl,
like dawn's first flame on a restless wing?
Don't let your spirit scatter
in the hurry of everything.

Where do you drift, bright leaf,
on roads you've never known?
Do you sense which way you've turned—
or has the wind alone?

Where do you sail, wild stream,
with stars still clinging to your hair?
A storm brews deep beyond the bend—

will you be ready there?

Where do you fly, lone bird,
with the nest still warm behind?
Your mother waits where pages bloom—
a quiet prayer in mind.

Where do you dance, soft echo,
with your shadow just begun?
Behind you runs a smaller song—
your sister, chasing sun.

So, listen, girl—yes, wings must open,
this is the age of skies—
But choose the wind, not just the flight,
that lifts and does not lie.

Remembrance

The canvas of blue sky where now
A fair of white clouds gathers,
Unmooring the cruel raft of memory
Adrift within my mind.

There again on the river's sandy shore
A flock of Kash flowers sway,
Again beneath the Shiuli tree
Gathering flowers, incense and conch shell sounds.
Somewhere, it seems, someone special waits
Eyes vacant, staring down the road,
Mind lost in the play of memories.
You are not before my eyes.........
Yet the Kash and Shiuli still whisper
your words.

(For you, Abhaya)

The Path

I'll vanish down the winding path
here blue pines wear misty veils,
Stroll through the twilight's mystic haze
Where Simul trees conceal
The sun's final, fiery breath.
The earth's stubborn grasp
I'll shed in river waters' gentle flow.
Arms outstretched, I'll drink
The open sky's pure light
And breathe the wind's raw truth
Deep into my chest.
In dusk's dissolving glow
I'll fade, a fleeting thought.
Then,
Reborn from ashes like the phoenix
I'll manifest on unknown shores.

Message

How are you, my friend, these days?
How do your heartbeats fall?
What joy plays the drum in your soul,
What sorrow keeps the beat at all?

Perhaps upon your rivered life,
A sail of bliss has caught the breeze,
And in that tide, your heart now floats,
Your spirit sways in gleeful seas.

Or maybe once more, broken clouds
Are dancing wild across your sky—
And in between, the fight for breath,
The dream to win, the will to try.
A march for freedom, visions bright,

still echo in your night and day—
How are you now, my dearest friend?
Do words still find their way?

Forest and Mind

When speaking of trees,
Many stories must be told.
Are trees just barriers to floods?
Stopping erosion's hold?

When a procession of trees is seen,
Clouds pause and stand still,
Then trees draw down from the sky
Rainwater at their will.

In pure, full breath of air
They supply oxygen's share.
In dry desert's doorway
Green saplings spread life's care.
Food, medicine, fragrance, and oil,

Countless gifts they bestow,

And they also offer flowers

Bakul, Champa, Ketaki grow.But trees' true purpose lies

In making a home in the mind.

Trees can make humans wild

Turning them to forest-kind.

In forest paths' solitude

Those who can get lost in stride,

Along the path they're able

Small trees carefully to provide.

Just digging a hole and planting

Does not make a forest grow.

To truly plant a tree

A forest in the heart must flow.

That's why I call to you,

Let's all go without a trace,

By the river in the forest

Laden with silvery Kash grass embrace.

Whistle in the Stillness

In the hush where thought runs deep,
the green of tea leaves softly breathes—
their scent unfurls like whispered rain
across life's quiet under-vein.

Golden petals gently fall
where shade trees make a silken shawl,
and by my feet, the fern-leaves lie—
their tender fronds, a lullaby.
Through every pore, the pulse of things,
a green, green life that softly sings.

Amid the haste of city tread,
the grind of days, the words unsaid,
a stillness dives beneath the din,

and from within, a song begins—
a whistle low, a deep refrain,
a green call rising through the brain.

The tea leaf—soft, like velvet skin,
with almond hue and warmth within—
it stirs a pull, a secret ache
the waking mind can hardly fake.

The heart—it knows, it always knew—
its final path, its turning view—
leads to a slope in a distant land,
where time lies cupped in a quiet hand—
a tea garden, kissed by rain,
with green, green roots that call again.

Torment, thy name is Prince

Who art thou,

The lonely wayfarer?

Meandering the harrowed heartland

Through haze of maelstrom?

Searching for the light of justice?

Why this tireless march through a blood-soaked soulscape,

With agony as your only companion?

The mind, ensnared in delusion's grasp,

Pierces foggy thought with a shrill whistle from the depths of

Subdued consciousness

Footsteps tremble, restless, as from vengeance's altar,

A shadow descends, creeping down Elsinore's walls,

Veiling even tranquil groves in searing venom's dark.

Through time's cloistered halls you tread, aware,

Bearing with you a burden of doubts?

Can you not strike the blow of reckoning?

Is all then falsehood, betrayal?

Endless stings of silence pierce your soul,

A thousand questions surge, unanswered still,

And nowhere, nowhere is the answer found.

Your footprints vanish into the earth,

Yet still you walk, relentless, down the road of disbelief.

One life, shattered by ceaseless strife,

Once grounded in trust that flowed like lifeblood,

Now torn apart by bloodied claws—of questions, of pain.

Caught between truth and falsehood, ever wavering,

Life becomes a tale of truth

Imprisoned in betrayal's intricate web.

For you, too, once knew love's flame—

A memory that still resonates, a heart's deepest string.

You etched love's indelible mark upon your soul,

Compared its beauty to the constancy of stars,

And to the sun's fierce, unyielding truth.

Yet alas, that certainty didn't endure.

It dissolved into murmurs of silence.

No trust remained in that love's fragile hold—

It vanished like a dream, fading from sight.

When awareness dawned within you—

Love's once cherished bond, immersed in the abyss of emotion was there too, alas! O my father!

Yet all trust ended in poison's gall.

And so today the spectral lament, anguished cry resounds.

The essence of existence, breaking the banks of life, flowing into the unknown.

Gertrude, you're more than just a regicide, mother,

You are the slayer of love, a betrayer of trust.

And so, night's ambiguity shrouds this nascent conscious soul

Ah, youth! Certainties now falter, uncertain and frail.

The light withdraws. O Earth! What toll does darkness extol?

Only silent thoughts grapple in a fierce, wordless tale,

Leaving scars in the air, marks of an unseen battle.

In love's fair orchard suspicion crawl,

Like cankered worm that feeds on blossoms all,

Till crushed lies he whose heart did sweetly burn.

And thou, O woman, turn—

To but a name for frailty.

No more, give birth to sinners—ah, no more!

You come to yield love's gifts back at the door,

Did you not sense the anguish that your lover bore?

Trust spawned a devastation beyond repair.

Alas, sweet youth!

Your delicate soul, a harp string snapped in twain,

Can't endure this agony, this unending strain.

Words, words, words...
Scriptures and philosophies erect towering verbiage.

Still, the enigma of this vast, inscrutable universe
Lies veiled in intellectual constructs, a labyrinth to traverse,

And lo, it is strife wherein the way is lost.
Cold-breathed doubts, like phantoms in the mist,
Bear up the soul's most dire perplexity—

A dread-laced realm, where poison dreams abide,
Toxic uncertainties choke the once tender core.
O Prince, thy silence thunders with revolt unchained.

In the inferno's swirl, ancient failures seethe,
Embers of memory, long smouldering beneath.
Love's lifeless visage you've beheld, and loss,

The mother, too, succumbed to death's cold grasp.

Why then, these sifting through shards of thought, with trembling hands?

Why, Prince, in silence you wear your grief?

In silent combustion, you've long been consumed,

Your resolve shrouded in the darkness of unspoken truths.

The calm has ended; the stillness is broken,

And from the void, a primal scream is awakening—

For justice, vengeance, and unrelenting might.

O heart, when will you shatter the chains of thought?

You've reached the edge; all is lost, all is bare.

Gaze forward—

Fate, a crimson certainty, strides relentlessly to claim you.

So,

Let it be—

The power of the chronal bow is now unleashed,

The time for action dawns, with strike and blaze.

Time's mark is left in on the arrow's head,

Poisoned and deadly, a fate already spread.

This kiss of steel conceals a secret sting—

Now, the footfall of death echoes near.

In the bloodstream with solemn tread,

The footfall of death now echoes near.

Hibernation

Silence rots beneath the skin of hibernation—
The hoard is fat with spoiled abundance.
A sickly festival echoes through blind caverns,
Pleasure—moulded and joyless—stagnates in its swamp.
All movement will drown in that sluggish mire.
The blaze of conscience, justice, pain—
Snuffed out, stacked in the cold pit.
The stored meat curdles, bloats,
Turns into something else.
Every promise made will decompose
Into the stench of once-savoured memory.
And while this sleep thickens,
A few vulture eyes still flicker—
Watching, weighing every tremor of dissent.

(For you, Abhaya)

Stonework

Scratching stone, an old habit clings,
Instinct drives me, again and again,
Torn nails etch lines, a stubborn refrain,
Blood smudges fade, yet I persist in pain.

In writing's tender ferocity, I hold
Sand and snow, embracing the void I'm told,
A bundle of emptiness, I cradle and mould.

Yeats whispered truths of crumbling grounds,
"The centre cannot hold," his words resound,
Did he hear stone shatter, silent rivers flow?
Tunnels beneath, a hidden world below?

Still, I'll anchor at life's core,

Where someday words will bloom on stone once more,

Cold, cruel surfaces will bear the mark,

A testament to art's enduring spark.

Seventeen Lakhs for Abhaya

—a lament

They bought her life for seventeen lakhs—
Her breath, her dreams, her sleepless skies.
Beneath the ink of folded notes
A thesis sleeps—half-born, denied.

Each blood-wrung tear, a crimson oath,
That testifies her silent scream.
A shattered pen upon a pad—
No balm, no hope, no healing dream.

They weighed her—litres, grams, and bones,
As if a life were measured so.
Seventeen lakhs. Just seventeen—

Enough to let a casket go.

The hands that held the fading pulse
Are fractured now by iron rage.
The heart that hummed of healing light—
Now stains the walls of history's page.

And justice? Bartered in the dark,
Beneath the gavel's frozen glance.
Buried where silence eats the law—
Bought for a corpse's last finance.

November 20, 2024—
A love-tale whispered, cut and scored.
Alpana dances in courtyard dust,
Vermilion bright on sandal floor.

A yellow flower in her hair,
A blue car trails the morning hush—
While in the rearview, ghosts remain:
Seventeen lakhs in blood and crush.

Longing In Dooars

Teesta lived

in the shade of my eyes.

Forests rose—

wild, wordless—

deep in the streambed of life.

In raw tea leaves,

green breath.

In that scent,

the rhythm of surrender.

Blue joy

took root in silence.

Keep me

inside your depth,

O river of illusion.
Let Mountain water
touch bare skin—
and cool
this waking mind.

Let me drown,
slowly,
in your soft sand.
Let silver shimmer
light the corners
of thought.

Let branches grow.
Let leaves fall.
Let my trunk
stand beside your hush.
Let my roots
anchor
near you.

Procession

A golden morning pauses, serene,
on snow-capped peaks, where light is queen.
On gentle slopes, where green hills sway,
night's shadows fade into new day.

In vibrant homes, on porches bright,
the transition unfolds, a peaceful sight.
A mountain stream awakens, singing clear,
its silver voice, a gentle murmur near.

Cool waters wander, mossy stones delight,
gazing, holding tight, in silent sight.
Through tea-leaf rows, where shade is deep,
tender silence flows, a soothing creep.

A girl walks slow, basket balanced high,
barefoot, wordless, with gentle sigh.

Step by step, the line extends its pace,
a quiet march, an endless, solemn space.

No flags wave high, no slogans resound,
no chants of power, no names are crowned.
Yet, they're the pulse, the quiet breath,
for whom Justice fights, in silent depth.

www.ingramcontent.com/pod-product-compliance
Lightning Source LLC
LaVergne TN
LVHW041307080426
835510LV00009B/896